The Cowrie Necklace
A collection of poems

Tikum Mbah Azonga

Langaa Research & Publishing CIG
Mankon, Bamenda

Publisher
Langaa RPCIG
Langaa Research & Publishing Common Initiative Group
P.O. Box 902 Mankon
Bamenda
North West Region
Cameroon
Langaagrp@gmail.com
www.langaa-rpcig.net

Distributed in and outside N. America by African Books Collective
orders@africanbookscollective.com
www.africanbookcollective.com

ISBN: 9956-728-75-6

DISCLAIMER
All views expressed in this publication are those of the author and do
not necessarily reflect the views of Langaa RPCIG.

Preface

As a work of poetry, this book expresses my "overflow of emotions". It is a portrayal of thoughts that seized me at one point or another and compelled me not to stop until I had penned them down; in other words, liberated them. From that point of view, I am an odd human being because I write at all types of time and in all types of places. I have become so used to these moments of "poetic pregnancy" that I always carry with me a pen and a notebook, even when I am going to the toilet.

The Cowrie Necklace is a collection of poems spanning a period of about a year and a half. I wrote the poems whenever the occasion arose. As a poem caught me and took shape within me, the theme or subject matter also began to form itself in me like a foetus in a pregnant woman. This book is the sum total of poems to which I "gave birth"

In my poems, I raise issues - some of them controversial. In some cases, I do not provide solutions. That is not unusual because when I write, I hear and listen to some little voice in my head which dictates to me what I should write and when I should write. The voice is so dominant that when I start a poem, I am not sure at the outset how it will end up. Although I may have my own little idea about what I want to recount, in the end things turn out otherwise.

The question may be asked as to why I am writing a fifth book of poetry. The answer is that when I write I do not count. Right now I do not know the number of unpublished manuscripts I have. I do not know where all my poetry manuscripts are. I do not even want to know. This is because, whenever I write, the intention is not to publish, although publishing may be the outcome. I just write and satisfy nature's urge to "deliver yet another baby". The truth of the matter is that each time I finish writing a book, I feel the same kind of relief a woman feels after going through the trauma of child birth.

The title of the book, *The Cowrie Necklace*, is taken from an encounter I had at the Commercial Avenue in Bamenda, with a pretty girl walking towards me wearing cowries as part of her hair-do. In our tradition, only wives of Fons (traditional rulers) wear cowries, to indicate that they are "royal property". So when I asked this girl and she said she "just wore them", I thought that was unusual enough to constitute a poem. The poem on her was written on the spot, although she never saw it because she was in a hurry. In fact, in the poem, I call her *The Girl in a Hurry*. Apart from inspiration from chance encounters, I am also inspired by my personal appreciation of people, places and things. In such a case, I can dedicate a particular poem to a particular person. Such is the case with 'Time Out', dedicated to Pamela Abeyie, a colleague of mine at the now defunct *West Africa* magazine in London. The poem, 'Equity', is dedicated to Baron Pienyam Teku, a childhood friend with whom we did holiday jobs at the Pinyin Area Cooperative Union. 'That which we Treasure' is dedicated to Ralph Awa, my English Language and English Literature teacher at Sacred Heart College in Bamenda. Mr. Awa demystified poetry for me, especially in Form Three where he dissected and laid bare for us, classical poems such as 'The Rime of the Ancient Mariner', 'Snake', 'The Journey of the Magi', and 'To Autumn', to name those.

Sometimes a poem originates from something I heard someone say. It could be, 'A Glass of Red Orange' as was the case with the poem by that name dedicated to Linda, "The Journey Companion" with whom I once travelled from Douala to Buea. On other occasions, when the urge to write a poem has grabbed me by the scruff of the neck, I have asked someone nearby to give me a short phrase, which I have then used as the first line of a poem done on and for that person. Such is the case with the poem, 'Life as I see It', dedicated to Rev. Sr. Ledwina.

It has not been long since I started writing what I call sustained poetry. My first attempts at poetry writing were at Sacred Heart College, Bamenda, when on two different occasions, I submitted poems for publication in the school magazine but they were both rejected. After that, I gave up. Poetry again tickled me some years later when I entered the University of Yaounde Faculty of Education (*Ecole Normale Supérieure*) and the girl I had fallen in love with, Florence, came to the same vicinity to attend High School. The compatibility between us was very high as she was a Cancerian (Water Sign) and I was a Pisces (Water Sign). One day during a visit to my place, I found I had written six poems on and for her while she was with me. Unfortunately, I lost all of them poem later, accidentally. However, I remember that the one I liked most was entitled, 'Her Majesty'. After that incident, I did not write any more poems until years later when while having a hair cut at a barber's shop in the *Parc National* area of Yaounde, my eyes fell on a poetry workshop announcement displayed on the wall opposite me. I was struck by the fact that the notice was not only calling poets but also lovers of poetry who would like to become poets. I went along and fell in love not just with the group, known in French as *La Ronde des Poètes du Cameroun*, but very much so with poetry. From that day, I was bitten and infected by the poetry writing virus. Today, writing poetry has simply become an obsession for me. I write poems anywhere and anytime. The person I hold responsible for that virus infecting me is the President of *La Ronde*, Jean Claude Awono.

I would like to wrap up by affirming that far from being a difficult subject, poetry can in fact be a treasure trove for the writer just as it is for the reader and listener. To fully appreciate poetry, it is not enough to read it or hear it. We must also allow it to speak to us. Poetry has its own language, its own rhythm, its own life, its own universe and its own destination. I thank all of those who in one way or another, helped in opening the locked iron doors of poetry to me.

Bamenda, October 2012.

Appointment

At midnight today
And no later than today
When husbands turn over and start snoring
And women looking for intelligent children fret
Roofs will quiver
And foundations will be rocked

The reason is that we are at the crossroads
The road our ancestors took
The one along which women too vulgar are punished
As things stand we have ourselves to blame
We must then make sacrifices
There will be no peace until they are appeased.

Time Out

I am the mid road man
I creep like the silent plant
Where I go, only monks enter
Where I sit, only king makers sit.

The thunder has shut up
The rain has ceased
The fire is going out
And you, you wear a cynical smile.

Don't take it out on me
I mean you no harm
I'm only a mid road man who creeps
I can never claim to be your boss.

Equity
(For Lord Baron Pienyam Teku, the man with the literary mind)

Let those who left first
Also pay first
For, never can it be fair
That some cut and run
And those who stay the course
And made to face the music.

If it was a matter of thirst
Then who doesn't know thirst?
Or is it that only those who dare
And do anything, even for fun
Must at all times and sometimes by force
Be given the Green Card and to boot, Swanzik?

That Which We Treasure

(For Sir Ralph Awa the Rover who made literature meaningful to me)

Oh, God of hosts
Strengthen each day our lines
Our defence lines
And help us to keep the bridge
Send the rain and thunder to the North
Not the south where we are
Those lines we carry
Come from our ancestors
And to us they are sacred
We shall allow no one take them
We shall allow no one defy them
We would rather give our breath
So that even if we are gone
These lines must remain
They must be here
Here at all times
To bear witness
To tell the tale.

Counting the Cost

Even now that I speak
The tide hasn't stopped rising
Already, the bridge has been swept away
Cutting us off from them
What we fear most is that
The rising tide may
Cause the fish pond to break its banks
If that happens, then that's the peak
Ten years hard work will come tumbling
Treated waters will be wiped away
Precious tilapia nilautica left without hem
Killed and flushed out for us wanton being to eat fat
It always happens in this dreaded month of may
After that we start from scratch and close ranks.

Who I Am
(For Lillian)

My name is Lillian
But I assure you, I'm not a Sicilian
I'm just an ordinary Ensabian
Who is also a worthy Christian.

I don't have much to say
Thank God you don't ask everyday
If you did, then no way!
What I believe is making hey.

Don't ask me about tomorrow
That will only bring sorrow
Let's take care of today and not borrow
Because wherever the Lord goes, we follow.

You may think I'm evasive
No, I think I'm very persuasive
Otherwise, why is every thing we buy so expensive?
Only God can lead us to what is extensive.

Liar

I heard him call her an idiot
Although he strongly denies it now
Expect that from men without a vow
Because all they know is the road to the griot.

At a loss

What should I say this time?
I feel lost and empty and sapped
It's like asking me to commit a crime
Otherwise, why forget the lines that were wrapped?

Freedom Day

All was calm on the home front
The curtains were drawn
The chickens still pent up
And the table set for three.

Then the strong winds came like a united front
And all the Christmas sparrows were flung on the lawn
Suddenly, the sky grumbled, went dark and we shut up
And a voice from above cried out:
'We have come to set you free
For this country is rotten'.

Memories

Do you remember the dance for two?
When as if enchanted
You and I drifted towards each other
In the middle of the floor
And everyone else, watching
Either scandalised or lost?

That was for me the first earned due
Thereafter I became respected
For, they all asked: 'How did he charm her?'
Remember the engaging ring at the door?
And the weeding ring worth more than a farthing?
Today I wonder what would happen if all that was lost.

Born Again
(For Ntembe Paul Amombi, the typical Aries man)

Let all the wealth I have in the world,
My gold, my silver, my diamonds
Go up in flames!
I don't need them any more
I have found
The truth
The way
And the life.
Let it all go up in flames
But let no one have one bit of it
Not one bit
Let some one else becomes
As trapped, as enslaved as i was
For so long.

Trapped

(For Mr Sylverius Mbuye, the unequalable secondary school teacher of ours we nick-named 'Agent de Terre')

The cry came from afar
It rang out once
It was shrill, sharp, agonised
At once we picked up our tools
And made about–turn
We knew that in these parts
Anything could happen.

Too bad I was dark and we were far
We knew at any time they could pounce
For it wasn't long since the last boat capsized
So, like typical examples of fools
We were prepared to spurn.
Although we had the carts
We lacked the fruits about to ripen.

Climax

Her shrill cry rang out
 And we woke up with a start
'Oh my God! She's lost it again!
Before I could pull off the loin
She was out in the night, naked,
Trying to catch something in the air
'What are you doing there, Ngwenyi? I asked
'They're here! They're here!'
'Who? Who is here?
'Can't you see?
They've come back.
They've torn up my post card
And they're tossing up the pieces
For me to catch!'
'No, I see nothing
No one, except you
In the sheltered light of the night'
'Well then you're blind,
If not mad!

Apocalypse

It was between twelve and one
When the silent birds had sunk deep
And the midnight song had gone hollow
All the forsaken beasts of burden
For too long left on the sidelines
Knew that come what might
The wedding bells would never ring again.

Now that I sit here brazen faced with a frown
I see the shiny necklaces creep and weep
The bride set in china on an altar made fallow
And the groom too lost to notice her all sodden
All of them lined up for a parade with no lines
What I failed to see, not being a knight
Were the huge cumulus clouds announcing the rain?

Conspiracy

I heard the tree branch crackle
And the Tilley birds in the deep night
Quarrel about the futile tattle
For so long condemned rattling.

Deceptive

I love to contemplate the moon flower
With its million branches
And annoyingly identical petals
They are the very receptacle
On which David of old placed his harp.

Hearing this you may say a flower is a flower
But at church, no two benches
Regardless of their uniformity in terms of rentals
Can serve as stool for the pastor's spectacle
The only real spectacle on earth is that which is ripe.

Cut It Out
(For the Rev. Fr Mac Mahon who taught us English at Sacred Heart College)

Get it together
By all means, get your act together
And save us all
From final damnation

Cut your Ts and dot your Is
Never again will you see the face of the Holy one
For, Jacob didn't live twice
So, make loose ends a thing of the past.

Flashback

It was not quite anger
No it was remorse
That was what made me do it
The emptiness, the vacuum.

Duty

When the rains come back
And the last queen fails to return
All kingmakers off track
Will run round the palace with the Fon's lantern.

Hold up
(The president's traffic jam)

Tell them the road is blocked
Tell them it's blocked at both ends
No one gets on, no one gets off
The search in on in earnest
There will be no let up whatsoever
Until the president's jewels are found
For how can anyone get away with the kings pearls?

Persona Non Grata

We shall not let him pass
We shall stop him by every means
We shall pour water on the path
To make it slippery
We shall make fire by the side
To make his eyes water
We shall dig trenches across the path
To make his vehicle stop
We shall plant a beauty queen on the way
To make his head turn
We shall stick the wrong sign post on the road
To make him take the wrong course
We shall replace the sign, kokala 1km with
The other, Kubota 17km, so keeps going
We shall do everything
So he doesn't pass here
He shall not
He shall never.
Never

Together like one

I am your brother
Can't you see?
I am your blood
We are one and the same
Same height
Same complexion
Same built
Same hair cut
Perhaps same date of birth
Perhaps similar names

Don't mind the different languages
The different dressing
The different greeting
It's the distance
The separation
The dispute
Not your fault
Not mine

Any way, that's all water under the bridge
It's the past
Gone, never to come back
What matters is us
We are here, in the present
We are the present
Bad may not be here
But we are here
That's life
So, together
Let's be one.
Indivisible
And move ahead.
Dad will know it
And he will approve.

On Purpose

I am out here
In the wilderness
In this strange world
In this no man's land
Far away from you and the world
Trying to make ends meets

Don't think I'm sleeping, as you wait out there
It's neither foolishness nor wickedness
If I didn't I would be hurled
Hurled by nature's invincible hand
I' am not God but I try to keep his word
When I return, expect the best treat.

Change of the Guard

I have played my part
Now is your turn
Turn on the lights for the real start
And let the midnight oil burn.

Reverence

Hold your breath
As the mountain god speaks
When it's all over and the drum beats
Scan the length and breadth.

Map Reading
(For my secondary teacher Mr Stephen Njong who made us love physical geography)

It's not a long and unbroken line
It's a contour with a centre point, but no crescendo
If you think the hunter's invocations too fine
See how his face changes as he returns from Owendo

Secret Agenda

You have no idea what he's up to
The kingfisher is watching the king
As soon as His majesty gets up
He will rush and perch on his throne.

Duty

Before leaving home
He took his eye glasses and his Bible
When he returned
He brought back the Bible and a stranded woman.

Precious Stone
(For the beautiful woman)

Shiny star of God's universe
How were you made so exquisite?
You alone stand out over in reverse
Do you ever thank him enough for this visit?

Contrast

The talk was empty
In fact, barren, sterile
We thought him petty
But he believed us senile.

Strategy
(For my brother Eric Ngu Mokom, alias ERIMON)

Be brave right to the end
Don't let them dent your honour
Face them with fortitude, like Saddam
That is when they'll capitulate.

Complicity

Let us together rise
Let us pull a fast one on the husband men
Let me tend the shrine
And you hide his horn
When he comes out for a drink
You will cry out
'My Lord, the gods have decided otherwise
No horn, no drink!'
Then will he die of thirst.

Trapped
(For the late Pa Albert Cho Ngafor, a man born far ahead of his time)

I know what to do
When he finishes his sermon and sits
I will rise as if going to ease myself
Then, within minutes
I will return with
The blood stained under garment
As proof of his infidelity
If he denies it
I'll ask him to swear on the Bible
If he admits it
I'll ask the congregation to forgive him.

Drifting Apart

It happens every day
Men without shame push their luck too far
Women without new locks and braids lay more traps
And the firmament moves further away.

In the evening when we gather to pray
We find that all the men are in the bar
And the women, although present, argue about wraps
How I wish for once I could have my say.

Conundrum

We are no saints in this world of today
But if the world were really our oyster
And every drifting pearl a globule
Then why on earth are finger prints not the same?

Question time
(For the ardent believer)

We all know about later day saints
And pride ourselves on our black rings and stout horse
But have we ever wondered alone or severally
Why poetry is speech that ebbs slowly?

Seething Within
(For Jessie Atogho Ekukole)

By every account,
Words were not what he lacked
But they came out poorly
At the wrong place and the wrong time

So he sweated like a failed mass boy
His scarlet nostrils sputtered ceaselessly
His feet were as heavy as lead
And his month was filed with salt and venom.

So Near, Yet so far
(For His Royal Highness the Fon of Bambili)

Over the misty mountain ranges
Lie a place no man has visited
It is a kingdom in its own right
With its own king, queen and court.

Deep in its mermaid filled lake of ages
Lies a chest of treasure recently re-sited
Alive and glistening by day and by night
It awaits collection through the inns-of-court

The problem, is no one in the palace is aware
Yet it lies squarely in the king's kingdom
If he finds out, he can burst a blood vessel.
Especially at this time of the year.

Who knows, perhaps while the village fool looks queer
God may in his wisdom and vision and dominion
Rekindle the light of Basel
Like the little but steady star of Bethlehem.

Same old tricks

I've heard it all before
Don't bother
Don't even think about it
Why me?
What have I done to deserve this?
If I want daisies
I will buy them myself
If I want jewellery
I'll order it myself
If I want a ride
I'll get my first horse
Not you
To me, you're just a missed fool
Who has for too long been mummy's boy
You need some growing up
But I won't be your nanny
I don't run a nanny state.

Uncle Sam

The lotus filled peach trees
Too tall for Sally
Are the angelic echo
I hear every night in my dreams
As I crossed the Atlantic
On my wooden bicycle
Bound for the land of opportunities
I may be mad to you
But remember
Every great idea
Started like some madness
I'm not reinventing the wheel.

Testing times

Oh! Where are you, my love?
Our love song rings hollow
So dear to me, it has today become a hollow sham
Everything I touch flees.
At night, the fig tree
The very one you and I used to sit under
Turns into a baobab tree
And teases me:
'If really, she was yours, wouldn't she come back to you?

Covalent bonding
(For Mr Forbi who taught me chemistry in Form Two)

Unable to bear it,
I got out of bed, fetched paper and pen
Wrote in blood my blood, the words:
'Here is my bond with you, a life bond'

The turning of the tide

The day I, in total disorder
Shall rise and ransack the room
Looking for the missing album
Even without asking you

You will begin to bother
And wonder if it's not the day of doom
You won't believe it's me Alban
All I'll say is: 'Shame on you!

My Lord and My God

When I think of how the earth rotates
I fall down on my face
And completely forgetting myself
I cry out 'Lord you are God in indeed!'

My Father
(Ode to my Old Man)

He went the way he came and lived
Queenly but profoundly
Calmly but brightly
Loving life but fearing God
Hardly calling God's name
But living according to his will
The day he died
Everything stooped to honour him:
The rains
The living things of the lower kingdom
Man
The sky
The universe
God.

Life as I see it
(For Ledwine of U.B., the place to be)

Life is not what you think
Even if sometimes it makes you blink
Whatever you do, just remember this
Pick up all your queen bees except the amber.

I have a heart as deep as the pit
It can also be one of the most lit
Although my love may be thousands of miles away
I will be as faithful as the queen bee of today.

For duty's sake
(For Mole of U.B., the place to be)

Life is not a bed of roses
And that I know from experience
It's not about my prurience
It's about doing ones duty despite the crosses.

Remember I'm the one with high standards
Never do I walk backwards
Always do I steer a steady course
For without results, one's simply off course.

Life's curious people
(For Diana of U.B., the place to be)

In life we meet so many wrong people
Some are angels, others in wolf's clothing
The Leo comes loudly, leaving many a ripple
She can stand controversy and loves storm stirring.

Dynamic, blunt and forgiving
She can nevertheless also chicken out
That's when she backs out without caring
And no forwarding address for anyone to find out.

Think again
(For Diterine the hostess)

You refused to be my guest
So let me be your guest
Let me in so that from these preys
I can cease to be a victim of pious rays.

You won't be mine
And I won't be yours
So I'm in the middle of nowhere, like nine
Is that a fair course?

Why should I a Soul Mate
Or so I thought
Suddenly, without notice, be fought
And made the second cross carrier with hate?

What have I done to deserve this?
I'm just being myself I n this home from home
So don't lump me with others from Rome
I have no hidden agenda whatsoever. So, why this?

A glass of red orange

(For Linda, the journey companion)

An orange, a glass and an ice block
A trio that may well read like a Chinese block
Especially on a Douala-Buea trip for five
In a corolla cruising without the bee hive.

If it's true about appearances
Then what about all the nuances?
And the half-full, half-empty glass?
Especially on the Buea lady of class?

I may not have spoken enough about the tale
But wait until we have to face the gale
Not even the tinted glass. Nor the black bag, nor the ring
No, none will be enough to remove the sting.

Which way?

Shall we sit or shall we rise?
I mean, when the master returns
Or shall we, like the Myanmar Saturns
Stop short, oblivious to the chant they prise.

Bolifamba
(For the Chief of Bolifamba)

This road is winded and tortuous
Even Hoptecs means little
Especially for locals less courteous
What more of the CBC's epistle?

That's why to flee the amorphous
I retire to Bolifamba for the epistle
I go there for the righteous
That's why my peace is far from little.

Together
(View from Mile 17 Buea)

We must cooperate
Forget the numerous street hawkers
Only heavy-laden women crossing the street
Will in the end sing the song of six pence.

Toad changes
(For Abraham Akum Mbony)

People change
Regardless of the range
But when the river overflows
Everyone must re-examine their toes.

The drummer boys of Mutengene
(For Pa Fritz Akum Geh of that town)

I saw two drummer boys
Both clasping a yam as they walked
Along the road from Mutengene.

Flanking it, they looked like wanton toys
Unknown, the invisible man stalked
But the drum wouldn't talk until it saw Nene.

Spot on
(For Joy Meyers, a former colleague at the Communication and Public Relations Unit of the London Barnet Council)

He couldn't have missed it
The great spotter he was
Nothing escaped his attention
Even the slightest speck in the remotest place.

That's why he spotted the digit
A figure the churchman thought he was hiding
Caught, he stood at attention
Until the catechist turned the figure into a big race.

Delays

(Warning from Church Street, Limbe)

What! Haven't you gone in yet?
You were here a long time ago
I've been to church and back
I thought by now
You'd be gone for hours
What a surprise!

I couldn't have gone without the net
That's what I need for my foe
In order to be on the right track
But first I had to make the vow
What our ancestors gave us as ours
To love and cherish daily before sunshine.

Directives

(On finding my way in Likomba, the futuristic city)

The first door on the right
That's where you enter
No short cuts, even if they look bright
The long ones are ether
And the short ones, slight.

The Sacred Cow

He didn't mean to
I know he didn't mean it
Problem is he didn't have his monocles
And he hadn't spied on the police boss
His shoes were mud-stained
And his left hand swung like a pendulum.

Don't take this for a joke from Tinto
No, for if it was, wouldn't I simply sit?
I have always read Sophocles
That's why we're never at a loss
I went to Ngaoundéré because I was retained
So forget decisions made because one is a hoodlum.

The stand-off

I saw the white ducks
Kick off their boots
I saw them send them in the air
And dare anyone to speak.

No one, not even the one with the bucks
Stepped forward to claim their roots
Only the passing mad woman stood to stare
That's why ex-players are quick to squeak.

The narrow path
(For Francis Selormey)

Blue tulips for breakfast
Are not necessarily bad for health
Not even when for the sake of clarity
One starts by reciting John Three Sixteen.

75. An evening with De Gaulle

I sat there wooden-faced
As if jinxed or even paxmanned
It didn't matter that I too
Like Ahidjo, like Senghor, like Houphouet
Was rubbing shoulders with De Gaulle
"Je vous ai compris!"

So near, yet so far was I
Hemmed in as it were by Verdzekov's rhetoric
And Bame Bame's implied philosophy
Here was I today with brethren
Whether from Samaria or Galicia or even Rome
To whom the overarching De Gaulle edifice
Meant nothing to anyone.

What mattered was the wine, the booze
The women, the misses, the near misses
The conjectures, the half truths
The half-baked projects
The vague promises
In short a future held on a distant platter
With nothing more than
'A face on which time makes but little impression'.

Magic tool
(For Oscar Nkamcho)

My Arab balm is all I have
And from it I never part
No, armed with it and a little tart
I can anywhere and any time, carve.

Tears for fears

I can't find the words
All I can offer is my tears
If only they could take away your fears
Then never again shall men be birds.

You as mine

Life means nothing without you
That's why I ordered a table for two
You are with me every time, everywhere
Wherever I am, you're in my sphere.

The rise I need

Take me somewhere
Anywhere, but somewhere
Hide me in your handbag if you like
All I want is a sure hike.

My question

Have you ever seen the pope?
Or are you waiting for hope?
And what if he becomes Godot?
Shall you then retire to Gobo?

Stale news

I heard him say that a long time ago
So it's nothing new
The only thing new is the forged certificate
Even his soiled boots are stale news.

Ebbing seasons

This device is weird
It has a funny way of wiping tears
It rises and falls, rises and falls
And in the end
The ebbing waters make way for
Gullies too deep to bridge.

To sit or to knit

For years I have longed for it
Just to keep fit
Wherever I sit
But what I won't do is knit.

Why I did it

No, it wasn't enough
Far from it
How could it be?
A few crumbs of bread
And two stale fishes
And you think that's a meal for a nation?
No! That's why I turned it down
I returned it to sender
And preferred to starve.

Later day knowledge

I didn't know that at first
So I mistook it for some birth
When I lost my way out
I knew I would also lose the bout.

Stopping point

I want firebrands that hum like bees
Not loose canons that thunder like Caesar
Don't worry about the hurriedly made sandwiches
Just let it rain when the yard boys come home.
Only then will the loud gun firing cease.
The elephant fight? No? Just forget it.

Torn apart

That was my final word
So I moved away
Clutching the wet and rusty handle
Through the toughened windows.
I could see the anguished, plaintiff faces
But between them and us
There was a gulf, a rift
A wide, unbridgeable gap.

Just then, the sergeant pulled back
And our fatalistic cavalry resumed.
Those chains were no major concern to me
What saddened me were the helpless faces
Those innocent men and women we left behind to die.

Only you

Life is nothing but drifting fog
That's why I paid for the clog.

You weren't there when I told him
No objection but just the odd hymn.

Today as I stand here
I am seized by abject fear.

Fear of the unknown
Of what a long time ago, I should have known.

Today, I'm finished
Like the sour food the old nun dished.

Right now, only one thing can save me
That's you and only you, sitting on my knee.

My dream flight
(For Sir Ralph Awa the Rover)

I want to be up and about
Like grandfather's old plane
So, let me fetch my wings
Before it rains.

I may be neither Gabriel nor Michael
But I refuse to work in vain
My wish is to dine with kings
That's when I for once will hold the reigns.

So, when?

When do you come home?
Now or later?
The kettle is on
And the soup is stewing.

But you may need some foam
From him who is greater
Don't think this is fun
Otherwise you may be yawning.

From the arena

(For my brother, Mbaku Christopher Cho, a gifted English Language teacher and a genius, who departed too soon)

There are times when
For want of something better
I stoke the embers
I do it on purpose
And then stand back
And watch the raging battle
Between heaven and earth
Between God and Satan
Between good and evil
Between the devil and the deep blue sea.

Narrow escape

I let it out
I let the cat out of the bag
But it didn't matter
For as he came out of the presbytery
He mistook the report
For the bell of high mass.

The obvious

Canon fodder and rift valleys
That's all he knows
Nothing more
After all
What do you expect from a mercenary?
With nothing but a weapon of mass destruction
A hood, a sharp end and a fake leather jacket?

37

The right time

I will start all over
But I will do so when the time comes
Not out of revenge or anger
No, but out of love for mankind.

Twisted fate
(For Ni John Forje)

I have never thought so
So, don't put words in my mouth
The landing platform is small enough already
All the idle birds have flown away
Away from the hapless Lords of the jungle.

You may take this for a joke
You are free to do so
But spare a thought for us the blind bats
For although you walk free
We are everywhere in chains, in bondage.

Spelling things backwards

Where was he going?
He claimed the milkman had just passed by
Making him lose a tooth
His favourite tooth.
But how?

He couldn't locate the prefect's house
Neither could he recite the Lord's payer
Even so, he laid it at the milkman's door
Do you think that's fair?
Just think about it.

Forgiven

I have freed my mind
So think nothing of it
I'm not a hermaphrodite
I'm only the corner store man's daughter.

Rooted to the spot

I will continue to stand here
I won't yield a single inch
Until the blueberry girl returns
She left early this morning
Wearing the scarlet dress
And carrying a national flag umbrella.
Unknown to her
She also took away my heart.

Bitter pill

I will go to the West Coast
All alone if it comes to that
I will walk tall, unbent
And at the lake side
Will I get a rock and with it
Will I provoke the water
Until it turns muddy brown
There will I wait for
The first basket carrier
And force him to taste it too.

Feyman

We knew it
We knew it long before he came
We knew his honey-coated promises
Were nothing but lip service, all fake
We knew his money was all counterfeit.

So when he came asking her for a visit
I said, over my dead body! What a shame!
When he tried to cover up his vices
At once we got out the rake.
That's why exposed, he went into a fit.

Far fetched

I didn't need salt
What I needed was Holy Communion
So, why was I offered salt?
Were they thinking of Christ's vinegar?
My God! What's the relationship?
Comparing a kingdom to an ant?

God's water mark

Today is a day of grace
So let's put our feet up
And lean over backwards
But let's not lower the flag
Nor let the grass grow under our feet
God's mercy is boundless
But can run out
Let's drop the masks
Above all, let's render to Caesar what's Caesar's
And to God what's God's.

My magic cure

I love red roses
Not just for lovers' day
But throughout the year.

They take away my crosses
And in their place, they plant a ray
So that for ever I can live without fear.

Short-changed

Finally I picked him up
He was crimson but looked golden
He was punished with a short thorax
And a disproportionate head.

Wondering what caused the mix up
I asked whether the leader was Roberto or Holden
Passers-by stopped not for the thorax
But for the buckets of crocodile tears I shed.

Wrong reading

He did nothing about it
Absolutely nothing
He just stood there and watched
Watched as the palm oil oozed out.

That's why we fell in the pit
And we did so without David's sling
When from on high the pastor watched
He told the synod clerk it was only a bout.

Hard-hearted men

No, it wasn't a question of right and wrong
It was a matter of life and death
A child lay dying
And we told him
"Where is he? » he asked.
"*At home, My Lord, very ill*", we responded.
"I want to see him first
I want to see him
Before I issue the papers"
"*But he can't walk, My Lord*
The child is bedridden, unconscious"
"Bring him, nevertheless
You know the rules."
"*But My Lord*
He may not get here
If we try".

It was two hours of pleading
Two long hours
During which my son's situation worsened
So we turned back to fetch him
To fetch this poor child
Victim of circumstances
Wrongly injected by a careless nurse
And now on the verge of giving up
This man could have helped
But he wouldn't
Just another corrupt civil servant
Always looking for bribes
Even if it meant short-changing life
And so it was we turned back
To fetch my little boy
We found him live
But weak, very weak
So with him we hurried along

We hurried back to the national capital
But also, it was too late
For I lost my son on the way
For no reason other than
Bribery
Corruption
Bad governance
Bureaucracy
Red tape
And medieval period methods.
When then shall we learn?
When shall we change?

The unaccepted prophet

He said it all
He said it at the General Assembly
He warned them that
Unless everyone paid up
The saved corn would not go round
For the second year running
Harvest was poor
Not enough grain
Not enough rain
But who listened to him?

Today was the day of reckoning
The day victims of
Famine, drought, disease and corruption
Came out each to fetch his share
But it was a wasted journey
The barns were empty
The rodents only partly to blame
They didn't heed him then
Now they had to pay the price
And a heavy one it was too!

Recipe for three

I will make it
Yes, I will make it myself
I will do so by hook or by crook
Even if it's not like at Unity Palace
What's so difficult about an omelette?

The secret is the recipe
Raw eggs, salt, onion, magi cube
Water, milk and vegetables
Then comes the fire and stirring
Lovely, isn't it?

Foul man

Another foul, just one more
And you are out
Out for good
Not even Arsenal will take you.

For years you have made the same noises
The same point
Standing on the same spot
Breathing the same foul air
Kicking the same old ball
In the same false direction
Hitting the same goal post
Thinking the same dirty thoughts.

There are too many fouls against you
Hand balls, pushing, wrong tackles and insults
Just who do you think you are?
Mister Big Stuff?
You're a foul man
With a foul mouth

Foul hands
Foul feet
Foul heart
Foul mind
Foul spirit
Fouled aura.

You foul anything
You foul everything
In the end you'll also be fouled
Because you're foul
Foul man
Fouled man.

An illusion

Shout it out on the roof tops
Tell the world all about it
Tell them you saved the world alone, all alone
As if nobody had done it before.

Are you saying Christ was all flops?
Anyway, how did you even do it?
Just because you made the Rome flame your own
You now think they have brought you afore?

Fair play

I have an idea
If she won't listen
Put some vinegar in a bottle
And ask her what's in it
If she says marmalade
Give her the yellow card
If she says Polish porridge
Give her the red card.
But if she says "market women"
She scores an own goal
And loses a penalty to boot.

Wrought iron

We were all alone in the boat
In the shaky tea room
What good luck, I thought
That the sun should descend without its loose ends.

I didn't mind the trunk calls from the moat
What irked me was the lone groom
For all I knew, this was iron most wrought
Peeved, I looked skywards and cursed the fiends.

Moment of pain

We shouted in pain as they struck
Paying no heed to the pelting rain
We knew in a matter of minutes
The sky would bury them.

Last wish

Take me somewhere
Not just anywhere
I want to see her
Before I depart.

One track mind

I hadn't thought about it
After all, what was the point?
All I knew was I was weak at the joint
That's why all I longed for was the pit.

Unacceptable

I got up
And went the way I came
This was too bad
A spoiled prince
Giving it all away
Just because
His ice cream had melted.

The brakes

Christmas is gone
And I'm sad
Fortunately, because I'm not mad
Otherwise, what would become of the fun?

Remember us

Thank you
Thanks so much for everything
But as you go
Remember to send back the lift.

The northern train

It was like a long meandering river
No, it was a long and winding snake
For while the river is constant like a lake
The snake is like a child gone haywire.

This was after all, Cameroon in miniature
For here in this extensive and tortuous life
Were all in one, north, south, east and west, spouse
Proud like the Lions who impressed their creator.

Here spoke loud and clear
Our great nation, unity being strength
Fulani, Toupouri, Bamileke, Anglophone, francophone
What a linguistic mix, my dear!

Family truce

I won't ask any questions
I won't even talk to them
Let them come in, queens, kings and princesses
And take their seats
Each before God and man.

It won't be doomsday, no, not yet
But it will be a field day
One on which any Tom, Dick and Harry
Can get away with blue murder
Ninety nine for the thief and one for the master.

Making choices

And there is one more thing
If you want a farthing
You must spend a thing
No quick fixes.

We live in a world of give and take
And besides, if you hold on too tightly
You end up by strangling
So for God's sake, drop the penny.

Of figs and mists

If only I had known
I would have done it differently
Even if it meant reinventing the wheel
That's why sidelines are sidelines
And fig trees, fig trees.

Today with so much water under the bridge
How on earth can I make amends?
If it was only a question of seasons
Then I would start with the mist
Unfortunately, in the world of figs here's no respite.

Impending danger

You may well think so
But how about the missed courses?
What if the armed forces
Returned and confiscated the manifesto?

True rumours

The wild rumours from the capital
Got there before we did
So when we lifted the lid
We found women who had gone mental.

My feet of clay

I was raised
But I was never praised
I grew up
But I was never brought up

My nothingness

I don't have a name
In fact, I don't have a person
The only thing I have is this old shadow
A ghost that has haunted me all my life.

Do you?

I don't know a man who does
Do you?
Are we together like some twin foes?
Walking up the wrong isle?

Not fit

Did you say you didn't like it?
Well, then you're not alone
If you don't think it fit
Then how can we send it to the Holy One?

The missing link

Where then are the cob webs
You said they were here?
What I see is an array of cockroaches
Trooping the colours before the queen.

If in the end the drooping lilies
Weather the raging storm
What will you say about the missing slings?
Or is it another case of weapons of mass destruction?

Still in search

We may be backward
But you're certainly not forward
When we find the henchman
Will you also find the bench mark?

End of line

I left traces behind
When the cow was shot from the hind.
The hoof marks you saw were mine
That's why we were at the end of the line.

Tell me more

I understand the life chain
But not the evil spirits
If you've ever tracked them down
Then sit down and tell me all about it.

The reason

That was all she said
Before the buckets of tears she shed
In the end, all the vicar said was
"He died for you. That's why you live."

The right road

Where's the road leading down?
That's the one we must take
So that anyone who is fake
Can experience the showdown.

Name callers

We're only sight seers
Unfortunately without sight
All we did was ask for what was ours by right
And hey called us seers.

A wing and a prayer
(For Pat, companion from the travel agency)

If ever I could see you again
And, believe me, that's my most ardent wish
I would want nothing else, not even a kingdom
No lipstick, no forward march, no tortuous queues
Not even Christmas carols or Easter puddings
For once I'd put off my computer lessons
And leave my unclosed poetry books on the empty deck.

If ever I could see you again
Then greatly would you make my day like the lone fish
My wanton life would go full circle, like freedom
Even Big Ben would refuse to take the queue
Birds would stop singing for fear of the new ducklings
For me off to Buea there would be a thousand and one
reasons
At last I can freely throw my arms round my neck.

Nature's law
(For Hilda the Taurean)

What comes around goes around
Perhaps not now, but in the long run, always
Life is too full of contradictions
Straight lines drawn in a crooked way
Eleven virgins running up the wrong way
What goes up must come down
And a banana that has to ripen, will ripen
Regardless of where it is put.

I may be nothing but a hound
If you think I'm reinventing new alleyways
I am only a microcosm among God's creations
That's why enfeebled, I look up to the father

He in all his might and splendour is the way
That's why when I pray, he makes my day
Before him, I can't frown
If I do, arrogant me, I stiffen
Knowing that what comes around goes around.

Off with a bang
(For Rika)

I'm going to the market
Not to see the Fon's ace men
Or to haggle over clipped prices
I'm going there to test the waters
To fathom the depths of the Upper Sixth
To gauge the value of today's franc
And to peg Capricorn expectations as expected.

I know the worth of the bracket
Even if it means nothing to them
Here where Mirabel the Leo rises
I stand and salute all mothers
In the family I may not be the fifth
But come August, I'll know my rank
That's why never will I be exasperated.

One step up
(For Mirabel)

I'm, not doing literature
No, I'm a social scientist. Just that.
And I'm a pillar of PCHS
I vow to it, my alma mater
I know that whether the world
Stands still or collapses like a pack of cards
It all depends on us social scientists
And our theories and policies.

I don't like winning by forfeiture
What I want is a pat
For that is what determines greatness
I have no goats to tether
But only my marigolds that twirl
I know not Paul
But I love Enrico and Mathematik
So for once, blot out all the 'ists'
And admit all those hidden fallacies.

My kind of woman

I like her hot and spot on
He must know what life is all about
She must have a pointed backside
She must come from Mars
She must speak fifty languages
She must be a mother of twins
And be prepared for triplets
She must have enough room in her heart
To satisfy this large ego.

Like a sister she must hush me
When I'm too loud
Like a nurse she must nurse me
When I'm sore all over
Like a true lover she must love me
Till death do us part
Like a mother she must mother me to the fullest
Like a grandmother she must dote and spoil me
And like the Holy Mother
She must forgive me my trespasses.
That's my kind of woman.

Woman as herself
(For Nicoline Bih, a journalist at CRTV Ngaoundere)

The woman is mother of humility
She is mother of father and husband
Whether you like it or not, she's here to infinity
That's why through thick and thin she knows her stand.

Right here at the Ngaoundere Independence Square
We are gathered by women and for women
Our women, resplendent in their attire are all aware
That on this day, all over, they stand before their men.

Women may not be the alpha and the omega
For that is the prerogative of the creator
But who doubts woman is king whether in Panama or
Bertoua?
That's why today, we all fete her as victor.

A woman is a woman, even as the girl child
That's why the world must spare no effort
To give her the place that is hers in society
Even Jesus came through woman without tort.

Eye of the storm
(For Irene Epie)

The heartbeat of Africa
All around the equator
Along the Nile
Across the Sahara
Above Kilimanjaro
In the minds of its people old and new
And strung together as one man.

That's Africa Bambata, Mama Africa
In a birds eye view, a snapshot as of the creator
Always motherly, never vile
Bringing all its artists together for the family palaver
But in that heart of hearts is Cameroon another Jethro
Africa in miniature, here to eschew, not to brew
That's why from refugee in Africa, he returned as son of man.

Life's lifeline

(For Mercy, the complete twin)

Life is a challenge, I bet you
It has the same stakes for all and sundry
No difference between twins and single births
That's why my twin brother is a banker
And I, a jurist
Yet like all of God's creations
We still find common ground.

Life is school whether for one or two
Lessons are already stacked like in a foundry
The phenomenon is intriguing, like desert thirsts
That's why I can't tell why I'm not a banker
But a jurist and a twin of a purist
Do I believe in reincarnations?
Well, yes, if only the clock of destiny is unwound.